W9-CLB-965

# Know How to Say No to Drugs and Alcohol

## A Kid's Guide

Written by Jim Auer
Illustrated by R.W. Alley

ONE
CARING
PLACE

Abbey Press
St. Meinrad, IN 47577

*For Noah, Ben, and any future, similar joys.*

Text © 2007 Jim Auer
Illustrations © 2007 Saint Meinrad Archabbey
Published by One Caring Place
Abbey Press
St. Meinrad, Indiana 47577

Library of Congress Catalog Number
2007928715

ISBN 978-0-87029-407-5

Printed in the United States of America

# A Message to Parents, Teachers, and Other Caring Adults

"My kid would never drink or do drugs. She's a good kid and she knows better." Sadly, such statements often fall under the "famous last words" of the "clueless," even though the young person may indeed be "a good kid." The opposite stance is also unrealistic: "I know he's going to try it sometime. They all do. I just hope he doesn't get hurt." No, not all of them try it; and simply hoping for no harm is ineffective.

Alcohol and drug education must begin early. According to studies, the average age of a child's first experiment with alcohol is 11. Marijuana: 12. (Again, this does not mean that all children inevitably try either one.) The message must be repeated regularly, but without becoming an irritating, continual harangue. Even so, adults can expect a "Yes, I know that" response. Risk it. Explain that important messages (like, "I love you") need to be repeated.

It's effective to use "teachable moments," such as alcohol or drug involvement in a news story or a television show. Asking the child his or her take on it and listening is more effective than immediately launching into, "See there? Look at what happened! That's why I keep…" Listening to a child's feelings, even (or perhaps especially) if they need to be modified, is important.

Some think success protects children from alcohol and drugs. Hence, the flurry of sometimes virtually meaningless certificates and everybody-gets-one awards. But star athletes and honor roll students become drug dependent, too. Conviction, strength of character, ability to resist peer pressure, and family support are far more important than success, especially success gained easily.

"Do as I say, not as I do" sounds hollow and often falls on deaf, or at least unbelieving, ears. The power of example is strong. "Teach…at all times; if necessary, use words," Saint Francis wisely counseled.

*—Jim Auer*

# On the Way to Your Dreams

People probably ask you what you want to be and do when you grow up. Maybe you already have an idea. Maybe you don't know yet. But surely you want to be healthy and happy.

People who love you want you to reach your dreams. God does, too. So they warn you about bad things that can destroy your dreams. Alcohol and drugs can do that—but only if you let them.

Remember the wolf who dressed up like Little Red Riding Hood's grandma? At first he looked harmless. But he wasn't. Alcohol and drugs are like that.

# What Is Alcohol?

Alcohol is a liquid. It's in beer, wine, and drinks called "whiskey" or sometimes "booze." These drinks are not like water or soda. Alcohol changes how someone feels and thinks. The more alcohol someone drinks, the bigger the change is.

Grown-ups are allowed to drink alcohol. They're supposed to know how to do it safely. That means not drinking too much of it or too often.

Children are not allowed to drink alcohol. Alcohol is more powerful to a child's body than to a grown-up's body. It's like the way some things are too heavy for a child to lift. It's dangerous even to try.

# What Are Drugs?

"Drugs" can mean many things. A drug can be a liquid or a pill. Some are put into someone's body with a needle. Others can be smoked.

Drugs make changes in a person's body. They change feelings, too. They can even change how someone thinks.

Many drugs do all those things at the same time. They might make someone feel excited and full of energy. They might make someone feel very relaxed, like in a daydream. Some help pain not feel so bad.

# Good Drugs, Bad Drugs

A good drug is one that a doctor gives to someone who is sick or hurt. The drug does things like helping with pain or fighting a disease. These drugs come from a "drug store," or "pharmacy." A doctor has to say that it's okay to take them.

A bad drug is one that someone uses just to make them feel like they're having fun. They usually cost a lot of money and they are against the law. Even good drugs can be bad if someone takes them the wrong way.

To understand all this better, we need to talk about feelings.

# Kinds of Feelings

Feelings in your body are things like being tired or being full of energy or having a headache. Other feelings are called "moods." Sad or happy, upset or peaceful are moods. Some feelings are in your mind, like being hopeful or being afraid. Many feelings touch your body, your mood, and your mind all at once. Being excited is like this.

Some feelings are fun to have. Others are not. It's nicer to feel happy and loved than sad and lonely. But it's silly to expect only good feelings all the time. It won't happen.

# Right and Wrong Ways to Change Feelings

It's OK to want good feelings and try to get rid of bad ones. But there are right ways and wrong ways to do that.

A right way to get a good feeling is usually something that you do. You might talk to someone you like. You might play a game, make something, or practice a sport. Doing something nice for somebody else is a very good way. It makes both of you feel good.

Putting alcohol or drugs into your body is a very wrong way to change feelings. So many bad things happen when children use alcohol and drugs that we can hardly list them all.

# Alcohol and Drugs Take Away Control

Alcohol and drugs change people's feelings and minds so much that they lose control of themselves for a while. They don't think so, but they do. They don't think about things clearly. They can't make good decisions. There are many words for this. Being "buzzed" or "high" are two of them.

Stupid, dangerous, or wrong actions look OK to them. They often say things they don't mean. Sometimes they commit crimes and get put in jail.

Usually they would never do these things if alcohol or drugs didn't mess up their feeling and thinking. Afterward, they feel very sad and stupid.

# A Big Word: Addiction

The more someone uses alcohol or drugs, the more he or she starts to want them. Without them, he or she feels "down," worn out, nervous, or even sick. This is called being "addicted," or "hooked." It happens much more quickly in a young person than in a grown-up.

Then more bad things happen. Drugs cost a lot of money. So a "hooked" person usually steals or does other wrong things to get money.

NINE OUT OF EVERY TEN people in jail are there because of alcohol or drugs! But at first they thought alcohol and drugs would make their lives better!

# Why Do It?

Lots of evidence proves that alcohol and drugs ruin lives. Why do many young people try them anyway?

Sometimes other kids tell them it's cool, and they want to fit in. It makes them feel good for a little while. Nothing bad happens right away. So they believe they "can handle" drugs or alcohol without getting into trouble.

Some children are angry about something. Breaking rules (like using drugs) looks like a way to let their anger out. Some children feel really bad about themselves. Alcohol or drugs seem to fix that, but they don't. Soon, they make it worse.

## Prepare Yourself

You WILL have a chance to try alcohol or drugs. At some time, someone will suggest it or offer them to you. Count on it. You need to be prepared for that. Young people can fall into trouble if they aren't ready when that happens.

Learn about alcohol and drugs. Read. Talk to your parents, teachers, and other good grown-ups. Listen to them.

Make up your mind never to use drugs. Ever. Period. Decide that nobody can talk you into it. The more you feel OK about yourself, the less likely you will want to use drugs.

# "Just Say No to Drugs"

You've probably heard those words. They're exactly right. But the word "just" may sound like people think it's easy. It's not always easy. "Just" means you don't have to say anything else. Just, "No—I don't do that."

You've decided not to use alcohol or drugs. So that's it. End of story. You don't need any other reason. You have a right to stick to that decision.

If others don't respect your decision, the problem is with them, not you. You're not the weak one, they are. Real friends never try to talk you into something bad for you.

# Be Glad for What You're Missing!

People who use alcohol or drugs will tell you that you're missing a lot of fun if you don't use them. Here is what you're REALLY missing:

- Always having to hide what you're doing.
- Always hoping you don't get caught.
- Hurting your parents, grandparents, and others who love you.
- Feeling bad because God created you for better things than drugs.
- Feeling trapped.
- Stealing money for drugs from people you love.
- Trouble with the law, a "police record."

It's very nice to miss all those things!

## Your Dreams Again

We began by talking about your dreams and plans. Let's end that way, too. God and everyone else who loves you wants you to reach those dreams. Alcohol and drugs are like an airplane that promises to take you to your dreams quickly and easily. But the plane always crashes.

Saying no to alcohol and drugs means you're free instead of trapped. You're strong instead of weak. You can be proud instead of ashamed.

Most young people are NOT using alcohol or drugs. You can stay free of those things, too. Ask God to help you. And then reach for your dreams!

**Jim Auer** is a retired teacher and the author of sixteen books and several hundred articles and short stories. He and his wife Rose live in Cincinnati, Ohio. They have two grown children and two grandchildren.

**R. W. Alley** is the illustrator for the popular Abbey Press adult series of Elf-help books, as well as an illustrator and writer of children's books. He lives in Barrington, Rhode Island, with his wife, daughter, and son. See a wide variety of his works at: www.rwalley.com.